The
Curve
You Didn't See
Coming

The *Curve*
You Didn't See Coming
Lessons Learned Through Loss

Carolyn K. Williams

Detroit Michigan
Printed in the United States of America

Praises for "The Curve You Didn't See Coming"

What a thought-provoking read, Carolyn Williams has captured the essence of healthy grieving and wove a great tapestry of expression and forgiveness in this masterful first writing. She takes us on a seldom-traveled journey and gives us tools to navigate a part of life, rarely acknowledged: the grieving process.

—Dr. Dale A Kates

* * *

When processing the loss of our loved ones, our spirits are often overwhelmed. Intuitive author, Carolyn Williams, uses her experiences in dealing with the passing of her loved ones to assist others in their journey to manage their experiences with death and grief. Congratulations, on sharing such a profound message of hope and inspiration.

—Minister, Pamela Riddick, M.A.Ed.

* * *

In "The Curve You Didn't See Coming," Carolyn Williams reveals that losing a loved one to death is not the end. A spiritual and reflective book about her own journey, it details steps one can take to recognize and reconcile losses. I was moved by it.

—Pat Barner, Grief & Death Educator,
Co-author of The Center Ring.

* * *

The 'Curve...' beautifully and courageously invites us into the personal and painful journey of the life and death of your loved ones. It is as instructional on the process of grieving as it is a heartfelt reminder that God never wastes a hurt. Death is inevitable, and the bereaved often times are not quite sure what to do when they lose a loved one. Carolyn courageously in her book honors the legacy of both her husband and sister. After reading her book, readers will have a broader understanding of loss and how mourning well is interconnected with living well.

—*Barbara A. Brinson, MSW*

Please note that email and journal entries were printed as written to keep integrity and authenticity.

Table of Contents

Dedication

This book is dedicated to those
who have lost loved ones.
I get it.
This is for you.

Foreword

Carolyn and I met in Ft. Collins, CO, at an educational workshop at the Center for Loss and Life Transition. We were tablemates and got to know each other as we debriefed what we were learning and shared our discoveries through some table assignments. Carolyn and I were learning from North America's leading death educator, author, and grief counselor, Dr. Alan Wolfelt.

Dr. Wolfelt presents a language and framework around the profound experience of grief that is so helpful. As students in this workshop, we explored the Ten Touchstones of Grief and learned about the Six Needs of the Mourner.

We discovered encouragement to feel what we feel instead of listening to society's messaging about bypassing pain, staying busy, and not thinking about the hole in our soul that appeared when our loved ones died. We felt first-hand the benefits of his Companioning Model. Dr. Wolfelt's workshops are a unique blend of a learning environment and a one-of-a-kind participation in a deep sharing of life's most painful seasons.

Carolyn presents to us in this book, how some of Dr. Wolfelt's concepts played out in her grief journey.

I honor how Carolyn takes her personal and painful experience commiserates with us and educates us as she recounts thoughts gleaned from her own journal entries.

In this book, the reader gets some insight into Carolyn's sister, Tonia; who she was, and what she brought to Carolyn's life. Carolyn also invites us to learn about her husband, John, and how she and John enriched each other's lives and blended their families in marriage. Tonia and John's life stories were both interrupted by cancer.

Love and Loss and Grief are all intertwined in this book of telling and reflecting. Carolyn invites us to post-loss growth and redefining who we are and who we want to become - but not until we have done the healthy, but hard, work of mourning. Carolyn takes the time to eloquently share some of Dr. Wolfelt's concepts, and how they played out in her life.

It's clear that Carolyn is a teacher at heart, inviting us to learn and grow right alongside her. She talks of others who stepped into her grief journey, providing some treasured gems, and words that were validating or offered comfort, and also reflects on some well-meaning people who offered words that were not helpful at all.

Carolyn again takes her own story and uses it to help us understand what words might be more helpful to present to our friends in grief.

Carolyn follows each chapter with Lessons Learned, and some Reflective Questions and then nudges us to the Action Steps that might follow. The format of this book might make it helpful for small groups or individual journaling exercises. A Christian focus is present throughout, with meaningful bible verses offered for reflection.

I appreciate Carolyn's contribution to the grief literature available. I imagine her words will resonate with many grievers. I hope your thoughts and reflections about this book will encourage Carolyn to continue writing, for she has much to give and many more to inspire. I'm looking forward to what comes next, and I bet you will too.

Patty Reis
Grief Educator

--

661-203-4817

Mending Hearts
Grief Companion

Certificate in Death and Grief Studies
Graduate of Dr. Alan Wolfelt's Center for Loss

Certificate in Grief and Trauma Counseling
Dr. H. Norman Wright's Grief and Trauma Studies

Certified Grief Educator
David Kessler program

Introduction

I used to tell people death was my jam! As a hospice social worker, I was comfortable with death and dying until my husband died. Then, I took time to sit and process what I was going through and had gone through with those I had been able to bear witness to.

As I sat, I reflected on the lessons I learned through loss. In conversations, I realized that many of us experience death and loss, yet we never quite talk about it openly or honestly with others.

My hope is that as you read this book, whether you are new to grief or experienced it long ago, you will reflect on the lessons you might have learned through loss and engage in conversations with others about your experiences, hopes, or expectations.

Although my losses and lessons learned are reflective of my husband and sister, I am aware that there are other significant losses one can experience: the loss of a parent, a child, a pet, a divorce, a breakup, or even the loss of someone you are caring for while they are still alive with Alzheimer's, dementia, or another life-altering illness.

As you reflect on the thoughts and emotions that arise as you read this, I urge you to write them down, process them, and talk about them with others. It is often said that we learn not in the moment but in the reflections that follow after a situation has occurred. My hope is that by engaging in this process, we can all learn how to grieve in a healthy way and ultimately live better lives.

Carolyn K. Williams

CHAPTER 1

When What You're Told Doesn't Happen
The Way You Thought It Would

So, where do I begin? With loss, we must take it day by day. One word. One sentence. One paragraph.

In 2009, blogging was a popular way to share thoughts. But my sister, Tonia Lynn Kates, wasn't familiar with it; she preferred emailing. When she was diagnosed with breast cancer, she told her friends through email. She had private conversations with family, and then updated us all through group messages about her journey.

She told me she dreamed of writing a book once she completed her treatment. I was excited and supported her wholeheartedly. Tonia and I exchanged ideas, sharing stories and possible titles. Naturally, I kept copies of all her emails.

But Tonia lost her battle with cancer in August 2012. My sister's death devastated me. The day after her diagnosis, she told us she sat in the living room, looking out the window, and saw a deer on the other side of the glass. It wasn't unusual—deer roam freely in that part of Cleveland—but at that moment, she said she heard a still, small voice tell her she was healed. We all took solace in that word and believed it to be true.

What I've come to learn is that sometimes God gives us a word, but it's our interpretation that changes everything. When she died, I was disappointed—even angry—with God. "I thought you said you would heal her?" I questioned. With time, I began to realize that He did heal her—just not in the way any of us had envisioned.

Once I moved past my disappointment and grief, I heard that still, small voice again: "Finish her book." I agreed — "Okay, I can do that"—and yet, I never did.

Fast forward nine years, and my husband was diagnosed with his second bout of cancer. The first was in 2005: a treatable but incurable cancer. He survived that one with little to no side effects—or at least, none he ever spoke of.

Then came the diagnosis of a treatable and curable cancer called "Large B cell lymphoma." The doctors assured us this was good news. But it didn't feel like good news four months later when we were told the cancer was like a tsunami, tearing through his kidneys and liver. Within those four months, my life flipped in a way that would have even challenged Simone Biles to recover.

When John was diagnosed, I began to journal my journey. He asked me if I was going to tell his story, and I quickly replied, "No, I'm going to tell mine." I wrote in the early mornings from my favorite spot: a leather chair nestled in the corner of our two-bedroom condo overlooking the Chesapeake Bay. Coffee in hand, I spent time with the Lord.

In the stillness of dawn, with the gentle sound of waves and the first light of day, I felt a sense of peace and reflection. It was there I often received what I call "downloads"—thoughts that were not my own. They seemed to come out of nowhere, but I knew better; they came from God.

Again, I was told to write the book.

I have three adult children: Jamaal, my oldest and my "number one son;" Nia, my eldest daughter; and Dominique, my youngest. When they were growing up, they often got into mischief or trouble, as children do, which sometimes led to discipline.

I'd ask them, "What's the life lesson you learned from this?" My hope was to teach them to reflect on their actions, develop critical thinking, and consider consequences before making decisions.

I remember Dominique once saying she was tired of life lessons. I wasn't sure if she was weary of thinking deeply or just tired of getting in trouble. Regardless, I told her that life would always teach you lessons—you just have to pay attention to their significance.

Now, I find myself in a situation where I have to apply the same lessons I hoped to instill in my children. I'm learning to pay attention to the lessons in the losses of my sister and my husband.

Lesson Learned

I've always said—and have been told—to trust the process. But I realize now that saying it is far easier than doing it.

Action Step

Acknowledge where you are in your process and be okay with it.

Reflective Questions

- Have you ever received a diagnosis about a loved one and anticipated a different outcome than the one that happened?
- How did you handle the disappointment?
- How do you cope with the loss of a marriage or relationship you thought would last forever?
- Are you caring for elderly parents?
- What lessons have you learned from these experiences, or are you still processing what happened?

CHAPTER 2

Tonia & John

*"It's hard to turn the page when you know someone won't
be in the next chapter, but the story must go on."*
—*Author Unknown.*

Tonia

Tonia Lynn

Dr. Tonia Lynn Kates

I n later years, she would become Tonia Stewart, and
then Tonia Florence, but through it all, she was my
big sister. My gregarious sister, whose thousand-watt

smile could put a lighthouse to shame. My ambitious—sometimes infuriating—big sister who knew when my younger brother, Dale, and I needed a push, always setting a high standard for us.

For five years, Tonia was the queen of the castle, reigning over her kingdom. Then I was born, and three years later, Dale came on the scene. Her Highness was not pleased to share her throne. Tonia was the first daughter born to Curtis and Louise, and the first granddaughter on both sides of the family. As a young child, I idolized her and always wanted to be in her presence.

When I was in kindergarten, and she was in the sixth grade, I asked my teacher if I could go see my big sister. When I walked into her classroom, she looked at me like I was a visitor from outer space, clearly unimpressed by my presence. But that didn't deter me; she was my hero.

Until Tonia left for college, she had little to do with me and barely tolerated Dale. By the time she came home for spring or summer breaks, I felt grown and no longer sought her attention. However, during "Little Sibling's Weekend" at her college, she invited a friend and me to visit. Her friends thought it was cool that she had a younger sister, and at that moment, the door to our lifelong friendship opened. Over the years, Tonia became my best friend.

With each milestone, we grew closer. She was the first to marry and divorce. I married, had Jamaal, and later divorced. She remarried and had Ben and Aliece. I then married John and had Nia and Dominique.

We spoke almost daily, regardless of the distance between us. During my nine-year tour in the U.S. Navy, I traveled across North America while Tonia mostly stayed around Bowling Green, Toledo, and eventually back to our hometown of Cleveland, Ohio. She changed jobs as often as she changed clothes, and wherever she went, people admired and loved her for being kind, compassionate, and full of life.

In 2009, Tonia was diagnosed with HER2-positive breast cancer. It was then that she started journaling about her battle. She began sending emails to family and friends, asking for prayers and support while sharing her experiences. Some of her emails were funny; some were not, but they were always truthful. We talked about writing a book once she finished her journey. Why wouldn't we believe she would come through victorious? After all, it was Tonia.

When she was diagnosed, Tonia said she heard in her spirit that she would be healed. She always had a special relationship with God and the gift of faith (1 Corinthians 12:9). If she believed something and prayed, it often came to pass. Some might say she manifested her reality; it depends on your viewpoint.

She even wore a button that read, "Give hope, believe, and expect a miracle." So, I did what little sisters do—I was obedient. I saved all her emails and gave hope, believed, and expected a miracle. After all, we had witnessed our mother, a 25-year breast cancer survivor, undergo a single mastectomy without chemotherapy or radiation. We'd also seen our maternal grandmother survive a double mastectomy, not to mention the many friends and coworkers who had overcome breast cancer. With a legacy of survival, we were filled with hope and determination.

Tonia's First Email:
Monday, 9 November 2009

Good Monday morning, Girlfriends,

I am praying that you each are having a wonderful, blessed day. I know this might seem a little impersonal; however, it is the best way for me to let you all know what's going on without having to explain it a million times. So, I ask for your understanding and patience.

I have been diagnosed with breast cancer. Without going into all the details, I will undergo a series of tests to determine if the cancer is only in the right breast or if it has spread. I will probably start chemo soon and will definitely need a mastectomy.

However, my spirits are great; I am a child of the Most High, and He and I have a covenant agreement that He is healing me as I write these lines.

I am only in need of your prayers and support at this time, as I know everything will work itself out. I have a wonderful, loving husband who is my strength, a wonderful family who is my strength, and I also have each of you to provide me with additional strength and encouragement.

Love
Tonia

(End of email)

After she died, I heard a gentle voice again telling me to write the book for her. I started but got distracted by life and never completed it. More than a decade later, in 2020, during the pandemic, I started journaling again—this time documenting my husband's battle with cancer. I ultimately lost him too, and the gentle voice returned. This time, I refused to let life distract me.

John
John Mitchell
John Mitchell Williams

He was "John" to me, but to his immediate family, he was "Mitchell." To close friends, he was "John Williams." When he spoke to you, he always used your full name, and to him, I was always "Carolyn Williams," said with a cadence that rolled off his tongue.

Everyone who met John agreed on one thing: he was a "Good Guy—" Not in a gangster way, but genuinely nice, friendly, and caring. He was laid back, someone who got along with everyone. I'd often say, "If you don't like John Williams, something is wrong with you."

John Mitchell was the second son of Richard and Clarice. He had an older brother, Richard (Ricky), followed by Wayne, and then 17 years later, Daniel arrived. The best words to describe John were "driven" and "funny."

Growing up in rural New Kent, Virginia, John knew his family was poor, but he was determined to change his story. After graduating from Old Dominion University, he bought a home with two of his fraternity brothers and began his career at Allstate Insurance in the claims department. It was there that our paths crossed— we met, fell in love, married, and started our family. John left Allstate to start his own successful insurance agency.

John was the father of our two daughters. Although Jamaal was not his biological son, he never called him a stepson; he always said, "This is my son," even though Jamaal's 6-foot frame and dark complexion made it clear he wasn't John's biological child. The rest of us were all under 5'6" and had fair skin.

John was the yin to my yang. He worked hard and played harder; I, in turn, played and worked. He was business-minded; I was people-minded. He was kind, and I was direct. His laugh and sense of humor were contagious; I was more serious. John had a gentle soul that poured into people, making everyone feel special. And I loved that about him.

Carolyn's First Journal Entry
Thursday, October 8, 2020

Our world turned upside down so quickly. I got a call from Dr. A (our primary oncologist) telling me to get to the Lake Wright office (the treatment facility in Norfolk, VA) ASAP. Dr. A speaks with urgency about everything, and this day was no different. When we arrived, Dr. A had left word with the front desk staff to allow me into the back room with John. Favor, right then. I noticed that out of everyone in the center, John was the only one with a "plus one"—me. (This was during Covid, so everyone else was going through their treatment alone.) I quietly thanked God for allowing me to bear witness to what was about to happen.

When we finally got to the room, the NP, Audrey—Dr. A's calm and soft-spoken opposite—told us John now had a second cancer lurking in his body. The first one was chronic, treatable but not curable. This new one was aggressive large-grade B-cell non-Hodgkin's lymphoma. This one was curable (Praise God), but it would require a hard-hitting chemotherapy treatment. Audrey laid out the next two weeks: blood work, port placement, CT scan, PET scan, chemo education—so much to do. I think when we both walked out, we felt like zombies, hearing but not hearing.

Since we drove separately, we called each other in the car:

"You good?"*
"Yeah... I think. You good?"*
"Yeah, I think."*

Both knowing we weren't really good, but also knowing we would eventually be. Both trying to protect the other but not having the words to put it out there.

Carolyn's Journal Entry
April 15, 2021

Been up since 5:30 a.m. Grief was waiting for me. Grief is an uninvited guest that has taken residence in my home. He just shows up as if he has nowhere else to go. It feels like I am in a boat in the middle of the sea, my anchor is the Lord, so I know I am not going anywhere. But every now and then, a wave comes by and takes my breath away. This is "new" for me—I'm usually the one who keeps things going. Today, my "keep-it-going" got up and went. Where it went, I don't know. Prayerfully, I'll catch up with it later. There are experiences I have talked about, but this is one I am now living. A new perspective, a new reality. They say God does not waste a hurt. Who are they? What will I do with this pain? I guess I'll share it with others the way people share condolences.

(End of journal entry)

Lesson Learned

Some losses take a little more out of you than others.

Reflective Questions

- Is there a loss that has affected you more deeply than others? Why?
- How have you managed to cope with the loss of your loved one?
- What helped you accept the reality that they were gone and move forward? Or are you still struggling to come to terms with their absence?
- Are you finding it difficult to accept that they are no longer with you?

Action Step

Take a moment to remember a fond memory of your loved one, then share that memory with someone else.

CHAPTER 2 : TONIA & JOHN

CHAPTER 3

The Curve in the Road
You Don't See Coming

"For I know the plans I have for you," declares the Lord (Jeremiah 29:11). This is a popular scripture many people know by heart, but we don't always comprehend that His plans may not line up with ours—especially when those plans take a turn we never see coming.

Tonia's Email
February 17, 2011

OKAY… that is my filler word. You know, the word you use just to say something. The word you use when you can't think when you can't really say what you wanna say, or when you're caught unaware. Okay, you get my drift. It's my word.

Anyway, for the past few days, I've wondered how to start this next update in my "battle" against that bitch of a disease called cancer. Make no mistake about it, I am in a true battle.

I thought I'd finished with this hussy back in November, as that was when I was done with everything. I had a wonderful Christmas and 55th birthday, and I'm looking forward to life.

Okay… cut to the chase… as some of you know, I've been dealing with this lymphedema in my right arm and neck. Lots of scans and tests later, and while the lymphedema is still there (no known cure at this time), on top of that, I've developed some enlarged blood vessels—collateral damage from the surgeries—and they've discovered a tumor in the midst of everything on the right side of my neck.

The good news is they won't be cracking open my chest… YIPPEE!!!

The not-so-good news is that my cancer has metastasized, and I've progressed to stage 4 cancer on the left side. OKAY…

In the last two weeks, I've asked my oncologist two questions, and sometimes, it's true: you shouldn't ask questions if you're not prepared for the answers. I do have what she calls a "life-threatening" situation, and on average, folks who have what I'm going through live between 6 months and 5 years. Well, you all know me, and I am not your average patient. It wasn't average to undergo "sledgehammer" chemo treatment, a mastectomy, and a flap transfer (the tummy tuck), and then have my body reject that and have to remove the booby entirely, followed by 6 weeks of daily radiation and chemo pills, and still have a year left on Herceptin. I mean, this is not your average stuff... trust me. And even if it is, I am still not your average patient! Therefore, I refuse, deny, and claim Satan as a liar with this "average" bull...

So now you understand the "battle" that I'm fully engaged in. I'm fighting for my life, and I am determined to win. I'm not only expecting a miracle; I'm expecting to BE the miracle.

I'm sending this email not just to let you know what's going on with me (okay, that's part of it... lol) but also to ask that you lift me up in prayer. I want you to call my name out before God and ask that I BE the miracle. I'm walking in complete faith that He will answer our request, that because of the covenant made between Him and me, I will be cured. My doctor told me to go out and enjoy life. Well, I am enjoying life—not because of this, but in spite of this. I am a child of the first doctor, the best healer, the true comforter, and peacemaker.

Okay... am I scared? Sure. Thus far, they haven't said anything about doing this one sober... lol. No chemo martinis this time; I'll be taking two types of chemo pills, about 15 a day. But if that's what it takes to get this hussy out of my body for good, so be it. Obviously, she didn't hear the "last call" that was her cue to leave the premises... lol. One pill causes diarrhea, and one causes constipation. Go figure!

I am encouraged, and I know many of you are already praying for me—I know this because it's only through your prayers that I have such peace, such calmness (most of the time). But hey, even Jesus asked His Dad if He was sure about hanging from the cross. I mean, I can visualize Jesus saying, "You want me to go through all of that for these folks? I mean REALLY, Dad?" And I'm thankful for my sense of humor.

Okay, this is my request to you all as my friends: Be blessed and stay encouraged!

Much Love,
Tonia

(End of email)

John was diagnosed with a curable cancer—Large B-cell lymphoma—in October 2020. His oncologist told us this one was curable, unlike the first cancer, Non-Hodgkin's lymphoma (Waldenstrom macroglobulinemia), which he was diagnosed with in 2005. That one was treatable but not curable. And yet, here he was 15 years later. So, why wouldn't we believe he would survive this one too?

Carolyn's Journal Entry
December 28, 2020

So, for those of you who ask and are curious, "How is John?"—It's an interesting answer. For the most part, he's tolerated the treatment well. We've come to see how most days play out. Usually, the first week is the roughest: fatigue, bone pain, headaches... just an overall crappy feeling. He hasn't missed a day of work, though. I think working helps him keep his mind off what could be going on. Yes, he's had hair thinning, but no weight loss, no nausea, or vomiting like traditional side effects, and for these things, we greatly rejoice 🙌.

But this is no cakewalk. For my husband, who is usually full of jokes and laughter, I see a dimming in his eyes and a slowness in his gait. For my children, who look to their father for his sense of humor and calmness, I see a sadness in their eyes and a quietness in their voices as they watch his every move. In him, I sense a weariness—not just from physical fatigue but from the mental exhaustion of not knowing which ache, pain, or side effect will show up today. And I sense his tiredness in having to answer my daily question, "How are you feeling?" when he can't quite put into words how he's feeling.

I've always said chemo kills more than cancer. But this is where our faith arises. This is where the rubber meets the road. This is where we are encouraged by the many prayers, where we find our strength—not in ourselves, but in Him! This is where we declare and agree that our God is bigger, better, and stronger than cancer.

So, during this holiday season—and this strange 2020 year—we are still encouraged. I am extremely grateful for your thumbs-up emojis, your prayer hands 🙏, your responses to this thread, your direct messages, your phone calls, your cards, your gift cards, your meals that have been prepared and dropped off, and your incredible hearts that have ventured alongside us.

Philippians 4:13 states, "I can do all things through Christ who strengthens me." But I've come to appreciate Philippians 4:14: "Yet it was good of you to share in my troubles."

Thank you for sharing this journey. ♡

(End of Journal entry)

Lesson Learned

When you think you know how the story will end... just keep living.

Reflective Questions

- What emotions arise as you read Chapter 3?
- When life threw you a curveball, did you duck, or did it hit you in the face?

Action Step

Continue to practice an attitude of gratitude, even in the midst of difficult situations.

CHAPTER 4

The Things We Were
Taught or Not Taught

My husband died on February 19, 2021, and my world has changed greatly since then. But life started to change long before he was pronounced dead. Early in October 2020, I received a frantic call from his oncologist saying he'd been unsuccessful in reaching John and that we both needed to get to the Virginia Oncology Association ASAP. I had no way of knowing that my world would never be the same. (But is it ever?)

Let me back up a few years. When I was five years old, my best friend's mom died after a surgical procedure. At age eight, my maternal grandmother passed away. Shortly after that, my paternal grandfather. And in between, my parents' friends and family started dying as well. When you're a child, and someone dies, there's a term for this: the *Forgotten Mourner*. Children often become the forgotten ones in grief and loss, as adults may not explain what has happened. In essence, they are left to process things on their own.

In our Western culture, we are taught as little people, then grow up to become big people, and never truly learn how to mourn. As children, we're sometimes told, "Don't cry," or "It'll be alright," or "Go play," or even "Don't ask questions." We might hear that our loved one "went to be with Jesus," and if you're young, that can leave you wondering, *Where does Jesus live? Can you go visit your loved one?* But then again, that falls back to "Don't ask questions."

Anyway, I digress. As I mentioned earlier, I was very young when I began experiencing the loss of others. Though death seemed to happen all the time, there was never any real talk about it, especially not to the children. While I grew up with the familiarity of death and dying,

I didn't know how to process the thoughts and feelings I experienced.

When my maternal grandmother died, I remember being at my uncle's house when my Aunt Norma Jean called and told him to bring my sister, my brother, and me home. When we arrived, my mother was in the dining room crying, surrounded by people trying unsuccessfully to console her. Aunt Norma Jean wanted to take us children outside, promising my five-year-old brother ice cream once she finished explaining what was going on. The only thing she said was, "Your grandmother is gone." Before I could even think to ask what that meant, my brother asked for the promised ice cream, and that was the end of the conversation about where my grandmother had gone.

Can you see where I'm going with this? Most of us, if we're honest, don't know how to mourn, nor were we taught. We're left to figure it out on our own, and who knows how that turns out.

By the time John died, I had experienced the loss of my parents, Curtis and Louise, my sister Tonia, both sets of grandparents, all aunts, all but one uncle, and several close personal friends and colleagues. Undeniably, that's a lot of loss. And yet, I thought I knew how to mourn. The loss of my husband exposed a pain deep inside me that I had no idea was simmering. It was as if I knew what loss was; I knew to be sad, and I even cried a little. But I kept moving because life must go on. And so that's what I did—I went on. But when John died, I had to stop, and the act of "going on" was painful.

When I worked as a Hospice Social Worker, I remember a case where an older woman was actively dying. Her son wanted to bring his eight-year-old daughter into the room to say goodbye, but his wife was against the idea. So, they called in the Social Worker—me. I spoke with both the husband and wife privately, away from the dying patient, to understand their perspectives. The wife shared that when she was young, no one explained to her what was happening when her grandmother died. She was told her grandmother had died, and the next thing she remembered was being in front of the casket, picked up, and told to kiss her grandmother goodbye. She recalled feeling terrified, without any explanation before, during, or after. On the other hand, the husband shared that when his grandmother died, he was simply told she had passed, and he never saw her again. To this day, he wished he'd been given the chance to say goodbye. He wanted his daughter to at least have the choice.

My suggestion to them was to ask the daughter what she wanted. To explain simply that Grandma was dying and to answer any questions she had. To let her know that Grandma was weak and probably wouldn't be able to speak, smile, or talk. And then, to ask her if she wanted to say goodbye, allowing her to make that decision, even if she changed her mind later. In the end, the daughter chose to go in and say goodbye to her grandmother, handling it better than her parents had expected.

Often, choices are taken from children because the adults in the room don't know how to handle the loss themselves—going back to not being taught when they were young. The intention may be to protect the child from hurt feelings and sadness. But is it really about the child? Or is it the discomfort of having to talk about death and dying, which might bring sadness to the adult or highlight that they don't know what to say?

Throughout this chapter, you may notice that I haven't said we don't know how to grieve or mourn. Unless you're familiar with the world of death and dying, you may think grief and mourning are the same. But they are not. Just because we use them interchangeably doesn't make it true.

Lesson Learned

Mourning is something we can learn, and it's never too late to learn how.

Reflective Questions

- As a child, how were you taught to mourn the death of a loved one?
- As an adult, do you react to grief in the way your family did?
- What's similar, and what's different?

Action Step

Write an affirmation.

For example: *I will give myself grace with the way I mourn. It's okay, and I will be okay.*

CHAPTER 5

GRIEF (I call it 'Bruce')

As I mentioned before, I wasn't unfamiliar with death, whether it was of friends, family, or patients. I often tell people—and still do—that death is my jam. I'm very comfortable with death and dying. However, after John's passing, I can honestly say that the grief and sadness I felt hit me like a ton of bricks I never saw coming. Today, I understand that while I had grieved (felt the loss and sadness) for those who died before, I hadn't truly mourned my losses. I pushed those feelings away and kept moving.

Grief is a natural response to loss. It can be overwhelming sadness, emotional suffering, an ache, or a pain—it's how we naturally respond to a loss. While it's often associated with the death of a loved one, death doesn't hold all the cards when it comes to grief. Grief can be triggered by many situations.

Think back to a time in your life when you experienced grief from a loss—one that wasn't related to death. If there were levels to grief, sadness would be the first, and grief would be the next. You might feel sad because you've lost your keys, but that wouldn't bring about grief—unless, of course, they're the keys to get you home, and you're now stranded in the middle of the road, with your cell phone locked inside the car. Yeah, that might cause some grief. But I digress; you get the point. Think of a time when loss caused a deeper level of sadness. That sadness is grief. And all grief is not the same, nor do we all handle loss in the same way. Sometimes, it's easy to shrug it off and keep moving, and then there are times we cannot or do not.

What we do with grief is called mourning. Mourning is the outward expression of how we deal with the internal feelings we're experiencing. Crying, talking, getting angry, expressing emotions, and acknowledging the loss and pain are all ways we mourn. There was a time when, after a loved one died, families would wear black armbands as a symbol of mourning. This band was an outward sign that a loss had occurred, reminding others of that person and allowing the "mourner" to be acknowledged.

Somewhere along the way, we stopped wanting to see, or be reminded of, a loss. We want the mourner to just move on, to get over it. And now I wonder if that's for the mourner's sake or our own.

According to *Dr. Alan Wolfelt*, we live in a "mourning avoidant" culture. We want to rush past this natural phenomenon of life. Why? Because our discomfort with others' pain makes us want to take it away. We don't like to see people cry, so what do we do? We hand them tissues and say things like, "Don't cry; your loved one would want you to be strong." Or, "Your tears won't bring them back." Or other well-meaning but, frankly, ridiculous statements. In essence, we take people's grief away from them, not allowing them to properly mourn.

I often tell people that if you don't deal with grief, grief will deal with you. Unresolved grief shows up as anger, frustration, hurt, shutting down, bitterness, resentment... the list goes on. You get the point. These unhealthy coping mechanisms will continue to haunt you if not resolved.

For me, grief showed up after John died—after the funeral. Before, during, and even up until the funeral, I had it together. Remember, death is my jam; this is what I do. When you're in the process of losing someone and in the days that follow, you go into autopilot—planning, taking care of business, keeping life going. But it's after the fact that grief finds you, sitting alone once the calls stop and people stop checking in. When you're left alone with nothing but thoughts, memories, and the stark reality that they're gone. *For real gone. Not coming back gone.*

There's a period when your brain goes into denial. Denial is one of the first defense mechanisms that helps you process reality at a rate you can handle.

For instance, think about a time when you received really bad news. Your first reaction might have been, *No, that can't be true!* It's like your mind needs time to catch up. The brain protects you, keeping you in denial until you're ready to accept the truth. Now, some people stay in denial for longer periods, which isn't healthy—but that's another topic for another book.

In my case, yes, I knew John had died. But one day, out of nowhere, a sudden feeling of profound loss seemed to creep into the room, and sit on the edge of my bed. It felt like an entity, and I was aware of its presence. So, what did I do? I let it sit. I cried, and I cried some more. Eventually, the heaviness lifted. I wish

I could say that I prayed or quoted scripture to comfort myself, but I didn't. At that moment, I knew I needed to feel what I felt—the reality of my loss. I didn't need someone to bring tissues and tell me everything would be okay. In my spirit, I already knew that. I knew that weeping may endure for a night (Psalm 30:5). And I also knew, "Blessed are those who mourn, for they shall be comforted" (Matthew 5:4). And if I didn't mourn, I wouldn't be comforted, nor would I be blessed. So, I sat with my grief—my overwhelming sadness—and I mourned, allowing myself to cry.

Grief would pop up again, and when he did, I named him. Yes, I called him "he" because that's how I identified with him. I thought of calling him "Bruce," but I quickly realized that if I told people, *Bruce showed up again,* they'd think I'd replaced my husband with a new man. So, for me, he's just Bruce. When he comes, I acknowledge his presence. I ask, *How long will you stay with me this time?* I'm learning to welcome him, and he doesn't stay long. When Grief is present, I reflect on fond memories of my husband and mourn the times we won't have together—the things he won't get to do, and the things we won't get to do as a couple. I acknowledge the things I now have to do without him. I don't throw a pity party; I feel what I feel. Then I'm comforted in my mourning, and my time is blessed. I move on, and Bruce goes away.

Lesson Learned

However you identify with your grief, accept it when it comes, and know that it will not stay forever. If it lingers longer than you're comfortable with, remember there's no shame in getting help. But seek help from someone who can sit with you and allow you to process your grief—without trying to take it away. Allow yourself to not only accept grief but to truly feel it. Do not deny it. Tell others where you are right now. Those who are comfortable will let you be; those who are not may distance themselves. It's okay to consider staying away from them when grief shows up. The more you do this, the better you will mourn. And when you mourn well, you begin to live well and love well.

Reflective Questions

- How do you deal with grief when it shows up?
- How have you been coping with your loss?

Action Step

The next time your grief shows up (and it will), welcome it. Sit with it, cry with it, and mourn well with it.

CHAPTER 5 : GRIEF (I CALL IT 'BRUCE')

_____

_____

_____

_____

_____

_____

_____

_____

_____

_____

_____

_____

_____

_____

_____

_____

_____

_____

_____

_____

_____

_____

_____

_____

_____

CHAPTER 6

Trail Angels

"There will always be a reason you meet people.
Either they will change your life, or you're the one
who will change theirs."
—*Mindset Creator*

During John's battle, I journaled my journey on CaringBridge.com. It's a website I learned about while working at the Children's Hospital, and it's a great way to share what's going on with those who want to know, without having to tell the story repeatedly.

Diane C., a woman from my church (at the time), read my posts and reached out to ask if she could pray for John and me. During our conversation, Diane mentioned that she'd recently watched a documentary about someone hiking the Appalachian Mountains. Strangers would leave things like snacks, water, or other provisions along the trail for hikers as they passed through. These strangers are known as *Trail Angels*.

A 'Trail Angel' is a term of endearment given to people who provide "trail magic"—acts of kindness and generosity—to hikers.

Diane then told me that during my life, both personally and professionally, I'd been there for others, which reminded her of Trail Angels. She said it was now my time to be on the trail and allow others to minister to me as Trail Angels during this season of my life.

I took her advice to heart and was amazed at the Trail Angels who showed up, both during and after John's journey. Often, they were the least expected people who would call or text. Because of COVID, not many people could show up in person, but some did. Since John's immune system was weakened due to the chemotherapy, we were very cautious about him being near others. However, if someone wanted to visit, we made the time to let them.

When my sister Tonia battled cancer—and I do say *battled* because it truly was—there was a lot to learn about what it means to face such a fight. When someone is diagnosed with cancer, they receive "chemo education," a list of side effects for each medication that will be given. These side effects are divided into three columns. The first two columns list the things that might and probably will happen: hair loss, nail changes, fatigue, nausea, and vomiting. It goes from bad to worse. And then there's column three, the one they don't like to discuss but must: bone thinning, damage to major organs, other cancers, and—of course—death. Who would think that the very thing trying to help you could, unfortunately, kill you in the process? Tonia mostly stayed in column two but dabbled in column three on more than one occasion.

Tonia's Email
July 2012

Three weeks ago, my pastor asked the question, "What does love look like?" I've been thinking about that ever since. Not because I don't know what love looks like—I have been blessed to know what it looks like, especially since November 5, 2009. I've been blessed with a family that shows love daily in what they do for me, in what they've sacrificed for me, in what they've given up for me. I know their fears and concerns with every test, every sickness, every chemo treatment.

For me, love looks like friends who have cooked when they don't normally cook (normal being the operative word). Who've shown love through daily cards, texts, emails, and even Facebook messages. I've felt the love of friends when I get flowers, and then more flowers when those die. I am embraced by love when family and friends are there for me 24/7. I know what love looks like when strangers are praying for me... I met one of those strangers the other day, and she told me how she has my name under her prayer candle... Praise Him!

I've never asked "why." Not why me with this cancer (because why not me), but why and what purpose does this serve? His response to me was that folks need to know what love looks like. A friend of my sister gave me a praise party... now understand, I hadn't seen Regina since my sister and John got married 22 years ago, but she opened her home in Chesapeake, VA, and invited folks—strangers to me—to come and pray and praise on a warm Saturday afternoon. Then my mom (not to be outdone... lol) had one of her friends open her home on a Thursday morning for a prayer breakfast. And again, there were strangers there I had never met. But they came to pray and praise.

So good family and friends, we are seeing what love looks like. I am constantly and continually humbled. I *earnestly ask that we continue to pray and praise—not just for me (although it is deeply appreciated) but for folks we know and those we haven't even met. We need to show the devil that we know what love looks like!!!*

I just want to say (write) that I hope you don't mind me sharing my thoughts with you in this way. Writing these emails has helped me in ways you can't imagine. I hope you enjoy reading as much as I've enjoyed sharing my journey with you!!

I know what love looks like when today I am reminded that my oncologist said, "on average" (average being the operative word) that folks with my condition live between 6 months and 5 years. I know what love looks like—my love for my God and His love for His daughter... because I am not average by any standards. His love, His peace that surpasses ALL understanding, His covenant... I know what love looks like for me.

Tonia
(End of email)

Carolyn's Journal Entry
December 7, 2020

When my sister was diagnosed with cancer years ago, she journaled her journey. One thing that amazed her was the outpouring of love she received during her treatment. Now, as John goes through this, I can say we've experienced an outpouring of love and support as well. So many people have called to check in on him. My friends have made sure we have food—they know cooking is not my thing, but they want to make sure John is well-nourished. Our elementary and high school friends have stayed in touch through Facebook, as have people from church and previous jobs. It's so comforting to know and feel the love. Amid COVID-19, people have still found ways to stay connected.

Thank you for your love, prayers, well wishes, and kind thoughts. I covet them again today. I'll keep you updated as well.

Thank you, 😊
Carolyn
(End of journal entry)

My sister and I have both experienced the blessing of many Trail Angels who came alongside us on our journeys.

Lesson Learned

Always be aware of the people in your life, especially when you least expect them. They won't always be who you think will be there. Often, it's the opposite. Some of those you thought would be there won't be, while those you never imagined will suddenly show up. But whoever shows up will do what the name implies: they will provide magic in the form of direct kindness and generosity.

Reflective Questions

- Who are/were the Trail Angels in your life?
- How did they show up, and what did they do?
- Have you ever considered yourself a Trail Angel to someone you didn't know? What was that experience like for you?

Action Step

Take time to pause and think about the Trail Angels who have shown up in your life, and give thanks for them.

CHAPTER 7

Please Don't Say....

It's interesting how, when you experience a loss, people often try to comfort you. Their intentions are good, but what comes out of their mouths is sometimes far from what they mean. And even if their words hold truth, they rarely help.

Now that I belong to the "Widow's Club"—a club I'd never want my friends to join, yet know they eventually will—I'm better equipped to know what not to say. Of course, widows aren't the only ones who hear unhelpful comments. There's a unique bond that connects those who've experienced loss. And no, all losses aren't the same; even among widows, the loss of your husband is not the same as the loss of mine. But there's a different level of reflection and sharing that happens. And a common experience is this: people unknowingly say some pretty thoughtless things.

"I KNOW how you feel..."

This phrase made the hairs on the back of my neck stand up. I wanted to scream, "No, you don't!" You have no idea how I feel. You may know the feeling of pain and sorrow, and you may empathize with my loss, but you don't know *my* pain. Why? Because it is *mine*. And yes, I might be getting caught up on semantics here, but trust me, after talking with other grieving people, these five words can cause more pain than intended.

Never start your sentences with "AT LEAST."

- At least he's no longer suffering.
- At least you're still young; you can get married again. (Often followed by, "Do you think you'll marry again?")
- At least you got to say goodbye.

"I didn't know he was sick."

As if that changes anything. Please say this to someone else—not to the widow. It feels like, because you didn't know, I now have to explain that he was.

"He's in a better place; no more suffering."

In my heart, and in my children's hearts, the "better place" would be right here with us.

"God needed another flower in His garden," or, "another soldier in His army."

As if God needs anything.

"He was so young."

Do you think I don't know how young he was?

Rick Warren, pastor of Saddleback Church, shared that when his son died by suicide, one of the best things people did for him was to show up and shut up. Sometimes, just being there without saying a word is the greatest comfort you can give.

Looking back, I'm not sure what was worse—those who said things they shouldn't have, or those who said nothing after John died. The ones who found it easier to avoid me and my children like the plague. People who had been a part of our lives for years but never reached out in any way. To me, their silence spoke volumes.

After John died, it was as if the world fell silent. The phone calls stopped, the texts with the praying hands emoji stopped, and very few people actually showed up.

On a side note...

I received a ton of cards sending "Condolences." It became a running joke among my friends. I kept asking, "What the heck do I do with all these condolences? What can I do with them—I can't eat them, cook them, or even smell them." My friend June decided to make a little jar with slips of paper, each labeled "Condolence," and every time something came in with that word, she'd put a piece of paper in the jar. A few weeks later, an old colleague of mine lost his mother. I wrote him a note, letting him know that I finally knew what to do with all my condolences—I shared them with him. So that's what you do with condolences—you pass them on.

In our modern-day culture, texting and Facebook have become the preferred ways to reach out and offer condolences. It's replaced picking up the phone or getting in the car to visit someone. Now, it's all about sending emojis: praying hands, hearts, kisses. But in doing so, it's also allowed us to remain distant from those who are grieving. We no longer come alongside them to help carry the load of sadness.

As I mentioned, I've experienced death both personally and professionally for quite a while. What I've witnessed is that our social media-minded society, along with COVID-19, has given people an excuse to avoid physically being there. For those who lost someone during the pandemic, their grief was compounded—not only by the loss itself but by having to grieve and mourn alone because others couldn't or wouldn't be there.

Lesson Learned

Before I went to examine the beam in other people's eyes, I had to look at the beam in my own. How often did I know someone who had experienced a loss, and yet I failed to do the very things that would have comforted me? How many times did I send only praying hands emojis? When did I actually pick up the phone, leave a message, or make a visit?

Experiencing the loss of a loved one exposes you to unique thoughts and feelings. If not dealt with properly, grief can make you either bitter or better. Bitter by becoming resentful, shutting down, and closing off those around you because they didn't respond as you hoped. Or better, because you learn to see things differently and respond with more grace.

As a counselor and mother, I often remind people that others can only give what they have. There's an African proverb that says, "Each one, teach one." If we all showed a little more grace to those who are grieving, perhaps we would all learn to mourn a little better. And as Maya Angelou so wisely said, "When you know better, you do better."

Reflective Questions

- What were some of the not-so-helpful things you heard while you were grieving?
- What were some of the not-so-helpful things you may have said while trying to comfort someone else?
- Were your words for their benefit, or for your own?

Action Step

The next time someone is grieving, instead of offering words of comfort, consider offering the ministry of silence and the gift of simply being present.

CHAPTER 8

The Other Losses

When one experiences a loss, we rarely talk about the "secondary losses" or what Alan Wolfelt calls the "ripple effect"—the losses that come after the initial one. Notice I didn't specify "the loss of a loved one," because, unfortunately, death is not the only event in life that can cause these secondary losses. But since I'm focusing on death here, let's explore what happens in its wake. Death is more than the physical absence of a person; it's also about the obvious and subtle changes that emerge afterward.

When John died, the obvious loss was that I became a widow—a woman without her husband. So not only did my husband die, but my identity as a wife changed to that of a widow, and my children became fatherless.

What does that kind of loss imply? John and I were a couple, and we did "couple things." We went out with other couples. Once a partner is gone, it's amazing how quickly those invitations stop coming—not from everyone, but from many. Either you stop getting invited, or you stop going. Suddenly, you feel like a third wheel, or it's just awkward doing the things you used to do. In essence, you lose a sense of who you once were and are forced to redefine who you will become.

As I mentioned before, I've experienced several losses throughout my life since I was five, but only the loss of my husband hit me like a ton of bricks, pushing me to redefine myself. When my parents died, I realized I could be considered an orphan—someone without parents—and with that came a loss of a sense of belonging, a loss of connection to the people who "knew me when." But I still had John to help me navigate those waters. So, when John died, I felt like a ship without an anchor.

I remember when my sister died, my mother expressed the intense sadness of losing her daughter. My mother-in-law, Clarice, said that losing John was the worst pain she had ever felt; she still cries daily, missing him. The loss of a loved one shakes you to your core.

You lose your sense of security—physically and emotionally. Now, I'm home alone. I've added another lock to my door. I no longer go to the store after dark—not because I'm fearful, but because I realize that if something were to happen to me, there'd be no one at home to miss me if I didn't come back for a while.

John was the primary breadwinner, and thankfully, he had prepared for our future well in advance. I'm blessed by how he took care of things. But not everyone has that security, and many find themselves left to navigate a new reality that includes financial strain and the loss of a previous lifestyle.

John also managed the money, so although I had funds in the bank, I was blindsided one day when my phone was disconnected. Turns out, that AT&T was not set up for automatic payment, and I owed $600 in back payments.

I've spoken to people who have experienced loss, and some talk about a loss of faith. They feel that God did not heal their loved ones as they believed He would. Others have lost faith in their church, feeling that the congregation didn't respond in the way they expected.

Lesson Learned

I'm learning to be more patient with myself and with others. I'm learning to do things I've never had to do before, or haven't done in quite a while—pay bills, change the battery on the fire alarm when it decides to go off at 3:00 a.m., schedule maintenance on the car, drive around the city, and reminisce about John and all we used to do. I'm recognizing that the loss of John goes much deeper than I initially realized. I'm learning to give grace and acceptance to those who could only give what they had to offer and learning to move on, slowly re-identifying myself.

Reflective Questions

- How has your life changed since your loss?
- What are some secondary losses you've experienced?
  (This can include a support system, identity, dreams for the future, confidence, or even faith.)
- What are some things you've had to learn to do differently?

Action Step

List some positive changes in your life that you are doing or would like to do in the future.

CHAPTER 9

It's Not Just ME

Shortly after John died, a very dear friend gave me a book by Dr. Alan Wolfelt titled *When Your Soulmate Dies*. At the time, it was too early for me to read it. I turned to the back, read about the author, and learned that he holds classes in Grief Studies in Denver, Colorado. The first class I took was *How to Be an Effective Grief Educator*. I chose this class because, in my experience, our society doesn't do the grief and mourning process very well, and I wanted to learn how to help others navigate it.

In this class, I met the most kind and compassionate group of 29 precious souls who had all experienced some form of loss. Together, we learned to hold sacred space for each other as wives, husbands, mothers, fathers, sisters, brothers, and children shared their individual stories of the losses that had shaped their lives.

Through this, I learned that amid my own sorrow and pain, countless others are experiencing loss too. Some from natural deaths, others from tragic events, cancer, COVID-19, and even death by suicide. (I learned that saying someone "committed" suicide is not the best choice of words; it implies shame and guilt, which only compounds the heartache for those grieving.)

During one session, a woman shared that when her adult brother died, she felt like a "Forgotten Mourner." I had used this term earlier to describe children who are often overlooked in grief. She explained that because her brother was married with young children, people asked her how his wife and kids were coping, or how her parents were holding up. Yet very few asked how *she* was doing. It was as if everyone had forgotten that he was her brother, and all attention focused solely on his immediate family.

When John died, I knew people would ask how my children were doing. But very few actually reached out to them directly. And while I was deeply affected by the loss, it wasn't just mine to carry. John left behind three wonderful brothers, a host of family members, friends, and business associates. My sister, too, had two incredible children—Ben and Aliece—as well as my brother and his family.

Lesson Learned

I once heard Pastor Howard John Wesley say, "Where you stand determines what you see." It resonated deeply with me—the pain of losing someone isn't only felt by those closest to them; it has a ripple effect that often goes unnoticed by others. It touches non-immediate family members, friends, cousins, and business colleagues—it closes a chapter in their lives too. Death has a way of expanding or shifting how we see life and its connections.

Reflective Questions

- Who else in your life was impacted by your loss?
- Have you spoken with them about their experiences and feelings?
- Remember, just because you're ready to talk about your feelings, others may not be ready to open up about theirs.

Action Step

Think of those outside yourself who were also affected by your loss. Call them, or share a meal together, and take time to process how each of you is coping without that person in your life.

CHAPTER 10

Reinventing Oneself After A Loss

For 34 years, I learned to be a wife. I learned to do things as a couple, taking on habits and traits that weren't necessarily mine but were part of being a partner. That's what you do—you tend to share interests, go to certain places together, and sometimes avoid doing things you might have done if you were single. Notice I said "some." You don't lose your complete identity, but you merge into a new one. The Bible says, "The two shall become one flesh" (Genesis 2:24).

The process is that they *shall become* one. It's a continuous journey of moving toward unity. In the 34 years we were together, we were constantly becoming one—not that we fully became one. And then he died, and now I am "one" alone.

My niece and nephew have had to learn to navigate adulthood without their mother's guidance, wisdom, and wit. My children are having to learn to live without the provisions and security their father provided for them.

And now, I am learning to reinvent myself. I'm doing things I haven't done in years. Is it fun? Yes and no. Some things are exciting and encouraging; others, not so much. I'm traveling more, going to concerts, taking classes in Colorado, and meeting new people. Yet, at the end of my adventures, I come home to an empty condo. There's no one to check on me to see if I made it home safely. No one to share my day or recount my adventures with. I'm still making sure the bills are paid on time.

But I've decided that while I may be alone, I am not lonely. I have old and new friends who continue to check on me. To move through my grief, I must keep moving. I cannot stay stuck. I refuse to let myself die while I am still alive. Though I continue to mourn their passing, I will forever be grateful for their presence in my life and for how they helped shape the woman I am today and the woman I am becoming.

Lesson Learned

Pain is inevitable. Growth; however, is optional. I'm choosing to grow—but I suppose that's why it's called *growing pain.*

Reflective Questions

- What are some of the hardest things you're learning during this season of life?
- How have you been able to re-identify who you are now?
- Do you like who you are becoming? Why or why not?
- In what ways have you grown?

Action Step

Make a list of the positive changes that have come into your life since your loss.

CHAPTER 11

Just when you thought it was safe.

"Grief is like the ocean; it comes on waves, ebbing and flowing. Sometimes the water is calm, and sometimes it is overwhelming. All we can do is learn to swim."
—*Vicki Harrison*

It's been over three years now, and I thought by writing this book and preparing to publish it, I was doing alright. I'd sat with my feelings, talked through my emotions, sought professional help, and did all the things I know to do—and have suggested others do. But one day, out of nowhere, Grief (or as I call him, Bruce) showed up and shut me down. I stopped writing, and stopped working on my licensure renewal—it felt like the grief was happening all over again.

Grief revisits us. It shows up and can take you back to the moment of loss. This isn't necessarily a bad thing, but you must learn to navigate those "waters."

There are indicators and triggers that let you know Bruce has returned. I want you to be aware of those triggers. When Bruce hit me this time, it was hard and unexpected. I thought I was moving forward, and in many ways, I was. But that day, grief hit me like a wave, and I became stagnant.

I was stuck.

I stopped.

I noticed my body.

There was a weight on me—I felt it in my entire being. Moving felt like trudging through quicksand; I was moving, but barely.

Another trigger was my eating habits. My diet took a nosedive, and I started eating more junk food. A major sign was disconnecting from others. I didn't want to talk; I didn't want to be bothered. I'm naturally a social person, active in my relationships, so this disconnection was a warning sign that something was wrong.

I often speak with widows and widowers who share how a song, a smell, or even being in a certain restaurant triggers a memory, pulling them back into the past as if it were happening in real time. It's a type of trauma, reminiscent of PTSD symptoms. You get transported back, and it isn't always unpleasant—sometimes, you smile, grateful for the time you had.

Helping others through their grief sometimes reignited my own. Feeling these emotions is crucial to healing. Because of my experiences, I've learned greater empathy. I believe God has allowed me to walk through various situations and emotions so I can relate to others. I may not know *your* exact situation, but I know what it feels like to be in a pit.

Grief is the same in its essence across all sexes, ethnicities, and ages.

Read the following statements. How many resonate with you?

- **"I go home, and there's nothing to go home to. I go home to an empty place."**
- **"I used to share my good and bad days with my spouse, but now there's no one to share them with."**
- **"What do I do now?"**
- **"Who's there to remind me to take my meds?"**

- **"Who will help me pay my bills?"**
- **"My wife/husband did everything for me. My role has changed."**
- **"My partner took care of everything."**

When roles change, you must learn to navigate the new reality. And not everyone is married in these relationships; marriage is not necessarily a prerequisite for grief. Having a committed relationship with someone you see as a life partner will leave a deep void when they pass away.

These are the words I hear in my group sessions. As a widow, I feel their pain. But as a counselor and coach, I must provide the tools to help them when their grief feels unbearable.

So, when Bruce revisited me, I *stopped*. I had to mourn some more.

The first time, I mourned for John alone. I kept moving, being "Professional Carolyn," checking all the boxes. But this time, I realized I hadn't truly mourned my mom, my sister, and the countless others who had died.

If you're a *Game of Thrones* fan, you'll understand when I say I kept hearing, *"Winter is coming."*

I wasn't sad, but I wasn't moving forward either. I was stuck.

For several months, I did nothing. My boxes remained unchecked. I tried to figure out where I was and why I was there. I visited my brother, and he spoke truth into my life:

"I don't know what it's like, but my hope for you is that you don't let your loss define who you are. When you tell your story, don't let that be your identity."

It hit me like a ton of bricks. An "aha" moment. *Don't wear widowhood as a badge of honor.* This is not my identity.

I sat with that realization for a while…

I am a widow, yes.

But I am also a woman—a single woman.

And it's okay for me to move on.

I picked my book back up and decided to publish it. This time, I am moving forward on my own. The first time, I leaned on others, which was okay. But realizing I can do things by myself is empowering.

It's okay to let go. It's okay to live again.

A relapse may occur—and that's okay. But recognize it, sit with it, and journal through the reflective questions below. And then, get up and keep moving.

Lesson Learned

When John was first diagnosed, I started journaling. My prayer at the beginning of the journey was that God would show Himself to me throughout the process. And every day, He did just that. Even though I didn't receive the answer I'd hoped for, He never stopped revealing Himself to me.

I am trusting in God's word. He has not left me or forgotten me. There were times it felt like He had, but those were just my feelings, and I know feelings aren't facts. He has been close to my brokenheartedness. God never promised that bad or sad things wouldn't happen, but He did promise to be near. And when I didn't think He was, He sent others to me. He renewed my strength when I was weary as I waited on Him. Today, I am able to trade my mourning for joy. I've learned not to fight the emotions but to allow them—however uncomfortable—to move in me, through me, and out of me.

"Blessed are those who mourn, for they shall be comforted" (Matthew 5:4).

Reflective Questions

- How are you feeling at this very moment?
- In what ways are you stuck in your grief?
- What smells, sounds, or memories take you back to that stuck place?
- Are you aware when other people's grief ignites or triggers your own?

Action Step

Check in with yourself daily. Give yourself grace. Journal often.

Not the End but the Beginning...

When I began writing this book in October 2020, John asked me, "Are you going to tell my story?" I told him, "No, I'm going to tell *my* story, but you're going to be the main character!"

Thank you for walking this journey with us. May you be forever blessed and encouraged, finding peace that surpasses all understanding—even when understanding seems out of reach.

A Prayer for You

I want to pray for you. I know this is hard, but it is possible. You can do this. I have, and I still am.

Repeat this prayer after me:

Creator of all that is, I'm grateful for those who have traveled alongside me on this journey, knowing that they too have their own paths to walk. As we continue navigating this thing called life, I affirm that we will draw on the inner strength, wisdom, love, and power within each of us and use it to bless and encourage one another along the way.

So it is, and so it shall be. Amen.

Acknowledgments

I'd like to acknowledge those who played a pivotal part in my journey, including my writing journey.

First, I'd like to acknowledge my husband. Thank you for loving me in the manner in which you knew how. You were an amazing husband and father. I will love you forever.

To my sister: Even in death, you taught me to Live Simply, Love Generously, Care Deeply, Speak Kindly, and Leave the rest to God.

To my children, Jamaal, Nia, and Dominique: Continue to live, love, grow, and learn the lessons that life teaches along the way.

To my tribe of friends and family members, as the writer in Philippians 4:14 stated, "Yet it was good of you to share in my troubles."

Bibliography

Alan D. Wolfelt, PH.D., Center for Loss
Howard John Wesley, PH.D., Alfred Baptist Street
Rick Warren, PH.D., Saddleback Church

Resources

We Grieve Differently: Podcast

Grief Refuge

www.griefreguge.com.

Center for Loss & Life Transition

www.centerforloss.com

Grief Shares

www.griefshare.org

About The Author

Carolyn K. Williams, LCSW, is a devoted mother of three, a loving sister, a cherished Nana, a caring daughter, and, more recently, a widow—embarking on a journey to find meaning amid life's uncertainties. In her debut book, *The Curve You Didn't See Coming: The Lessons I Learned Through the Loss of a Loved One*, she shares profound insights and

hard-earned wisdom from her experiences with loss and grief.

A proud resident of Virginia Beach, VA, Carolyn is a beloved member of her community. Her passion for theater, love of engaging conversations, and enthusiasm for dancing infuse her life with vibrant energy and joy. Her compassionate spirit and open heart are evident in her writing, offering hope and guidance to those grappling with the complexities of grief. Carolyn's book stands as a beacon of resilience, demonstrating her unwavering commitment to helping others navigate their own journeys through loss.

You don't have to walk this walk alone.

Contact Me:

Website: www.mourningwell.com

Contact: carolynkwilliams@gmail.com